# THE RE PEREGRINE FALCON

MW01006899

## BY SUSAN BLACKABY

Harcourt

Orlando   Boston   Dallas   Chicago   San Diego

Visit *The Learning Site!*

**www.harcourtschool.com**

DDT is a poison that was made to get rid of pests. It was used in the United States years ago. It killed insects that can make you sick when they sting you. DDT seemed like a good thing, but it caused bad things to happen.

DDT got into the streams and the soil as well as on the insects. Living things that ate and drank food and water had DDT in them. The DDT stayed in their bodies.

It is typical for small birds to eat bugs. It is typical for some large birds to eat small birds. When small birds ate insects sprayed with DDT, the DDT got into the birds' bodies. When large birds ate the small birds, the DDT got into their bodies, too.

At first, scientists did not know that DDT could harm birds. Then peregrine falcons began to die. Scientists wondered if all the peregrine falcons would die. Something had to be done to save them.

For those falcons that lived, the DDT in their bodies caused other problems. When the females laid eggs, the shells were very thin. The eggs cracked when the mother birds sat on them. The chicks were not fully formed, and they died.

People were confused about what could have caused this problem. As the years went by, it looked as if the falcons were going to die out.

Scientists studied the falcons' eggshells to see what was going on. They discovered that the thin shells had a lot of DDT in them. The DDT caused the shells to dry out and crack. The DDT was the problem.

The scientists prepared to save the falcons. "Here is the plan," they said. Somebody goes up the face of the cliff and removes the eggs from the nest."

The scientists did not want to be cornered by angry mother birds. They waited for them to leave before picking the eggs from the nests. They replaced them with objects that looked like the real eggs. The mother birds could sit on these while the real eggs went to a lab.

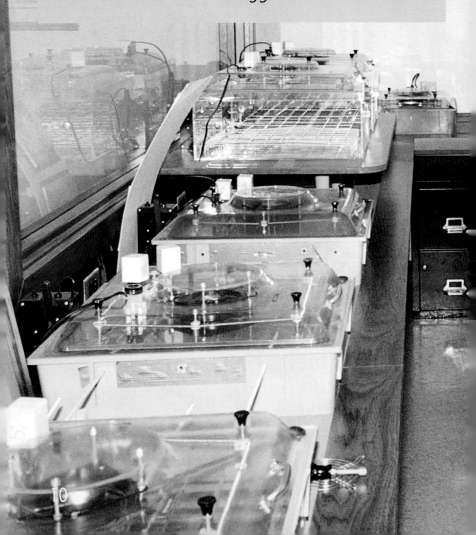

Scientists put the eggs in an incubator that was kept shut with a clasp. They mended the cracks in the shells. They kept the shells wet so the chicks would not dry out. They turned the eggs over and over. The chicks could not hatch without this special care.

When the chicks hatched, the scientists fed them using puppets that looked like mother birds. They didn't want them to depend on people for food. After three weeks, they returned the chicks to the nest and removed the fake eggs. The parent birds fed the chicks until they were grown.

However, the chicks were still not safe. They, too, might eat small birds that ate bugs sprayed with DDT. Then their eggs would also have thin shells. The problem would go on and on! To prevent this, people had to stop using DDT.

To get rid of DDT, the U.S. government passed a law against using it. In some parts of the world, however, DDT is still used to kill pests.

Getting rid of DDT takes a long time. Many years after people stopped using DDT, some falcons still needed help.

Today, small amounts of DDT can still be found, but most falcons live without help. Scientists keep track of the birds. They check the shells of their eggs to see if they are strong.

The peregrine falcon nearly died out in parts of the United States. Other birds, such as eagles, were also harmed by DDT.

Asking the right questions and working hard to solve the problem saved the birds. The peregrine falcons soar strong and safe once again.